EXPLORING
The Solar System

by Colleen Sexton

Consultant:
Duane Quam, M.S. Physics
Chair, Minnesota State
Academic Science Standards
Writing Committee

BLASTOFF! READERS
3

BELLWETHER MEDIA • MINNEAPOLIS, MN

Note to Librarians, Teachers, and Parents:

Blastoff! Readers are carefully developed by literacy experts and combine standards-based content with developmentally appropriate text.

Level 1 provides the most support through repetition of high-frequency words, light text, predictable sentence patterns, and strong visual support.

Level 2 offers early readers a bit more challenge through varied simple sentences, increased text load, and less repetition of high-frequency words.

Level 3 advances early-fluent readers toward fluency through increased text and concept load, less reliance on visuals, longer sentences, and more literary language.

Level 4 builds reading stamina by providing more text per page, increased use of punctuation, greater variation in sentence patterns, and increasingly challenging vocabulary.

Level 5 encourages children to move from "learning to read" to "reading to learn" by providing even more text, varied writing styles, and less familiar topics.

Whichever book is right for your reader, Blastoff! Readers are the perfect books to build confidence and encourage a love of reading that will last a lifetime!

This edition first published in 2016 by Bellwether Media, Inc.

No part of this publication may be reproduced in whole or in part without written permission of the publisher. For information regarding permission, write to Bellwether Media, Inc., Attention: Permissions Department, 6012 Blue Circle Dr., Minnetonka, MN 55343.

Library of Congress Cataloging-in-Publication Data

Sexton, Colleen A., 1967-
  The solar system / by Colleen Sexton.
     p. cm. – (Blastoff! Readers. Exploring space)
  Includes bibliographical references and index.
  Summary: "Introductory text and full-color images explore the physical characteristics and discovery of the solar system. Intended for students in kindergarten through third grade"–Provided by publisher.
  ISBN: 978-1-60014-411-0 (hardcover : alk. paper)
  ISBN: 978-1-62617-487-0 (paperback : alk. paper)
  1. Solar system–Juvenile literature. I. Title.
  QB501.3.S49 2010
  523.2–dc22   2009038027

Contents

The solar system is the sun and all the objects that move around it.

The sun is a **star** that gives off light and heat. It is the largest object in the solar system.

The sun's **gravity** is strong.
It pulls on the surrounding objects
so they do not move away.

There are eight **planets** in the solar system. Each planet travels around the sun in its own **orbit**.

Mercury

Mercury is a rocky planet that moves fast. It zooms through space at 104,000 miles (167,000 kilometers) per hour!

Venus is the planet with the hottest surface. It has a thick **atmosphere** that holds in the sun's heat.

Venus

Earth

Earth is just the right distance from the sun. It is not too hot or too cold. People, animals, and plants can live on Earth.

Mars is a cold, red-brown planet. It has plains and canyons. Melted rock called lava once flowed from the planet's huge **volcanoes**.

Mars

Jupiter, Saturn, Uranus, and Neptune are the planets farthest from the sun. These giant, cold planets are made of gases.

Jupiter

Saturn

Uranus

Neptune

Rings made of rocks, dust, and ice circle each of the giant gas planets.

Dwarf planets are smaller than planets and share their orbits with other objects.

Eris

Pluto

Ceres

Eris, Pluto, and Ceres are some of the dwarf planets in the solar system. They are made of rock and ice.

the moon

Moons are objects that travel around planets and dwarf planets. Earth's moon is one of more than 300 moons in the solar system.

Millions of **asteroids** circle the sun between Mars and Jupiter. These large space rocks can be hundreds of miles wide.

comet

Comets make long, oval orbits around the sun. These small balls of ice and dust have glowing tails of gases when they are near the sun.

Pieces of asteroids and comets are **meteoroids**. Meteoroids that reach Earth heat up and glow as they fall through the atmosphere.

meteoroid

space telescope

Astronomers use powerful **space telescopes**. The telescopes can take pictures of objects beyond our solar system.

Astronomers are searching for other solar systems. They hope to find a planet like Earth.

Glossary

asteroids—space rocks that orbit the sun

astronomers—scientists who study space and objects in space

atmosphere—the gases around an object in space

comets—space objects made of ice, dust, and gases that orbit the sun

dwarf planets—round space objects that orbit the sun and are not moons; dwarf planets share their orbits with other large space objects.

gravity—the force that pulls objects toward each other; gravity keeps objects from moving away into space.

meteoroids—pieces of asteroids and comets that orbit the sun

orbit—to travel around the sun or other object in space

planets—large, round space objects that orbit the sun and are alone in their orbits

space telescopes—telescopes that take images from above the atmosphere

star—a large ball of burning gases in space; the sun is a star.

volcanoes—holes in a planet's surface through which melted rock called lava flows; over time the lava can form a mountain.

To Learn More

AT THE LIBRARY
Bredeson, Carmen. *What Is the Solar System?*
Berkeley Heights, N.J.: Enslow Elementary, 2008.

Goldsmith, Mike. *Solar System*. Boston, Mass.:
Kingfisher, 2004.

Simon, Seymour. *Our Solar System*. New York, N.Y.:
Collins, 2007.

ON THE WEB
Learning more about
the solar system is as easy as 1, 2, 3.

1. Go to www.factsurfer.com.

2. Enter "solar system" into the search box.

3. Click the "Surf" button and you will see a list of
   related Web sites.

With factsurfer.com, finding more information is just a
click away.

BLASTOFF! JIMMY CHALLENGE
Blastoff! Jimmy is hidden somewhere in this book.
Can you find him? If you need help, you can find a
hint at the bottom of page 24.

Index

The images in this book are reproduced through the courtesy of: Mark Garlick / Alamy, front cover; Detlev van Ravenswaay / Photo Researchers, Inc., pp. 4-5; NASA, pp. 6-7, 16, 17, 20, 21; Christian Darkin / Photo Researchers, Inc., p. 8; Byron W. Moore, pp. 8 (small), 9 (small), 11 (small); Julian Baum / Photo Researchers, Inc., p. 9; Paul Paladin, p. 10; Juan Martinez, pp. 10 (small), 18-19; Detlef van Ravenswaay, p.11; Juan Eppardo, pp. 12-13; Mark Garlick / Photo Researchers, Inc., pp. 13 (small), 14-15; Giovanni Benintende, p. 18 (small).

Blastoff! Jimmy Challenge (from page 23).
Hint: Go to page 20 and "scope" it out.